THE ORIGINAL UK SLOW COOKER RECIPE BOOK

Delicious Recipes That Prep Fast And Cook Slow For The Whole Family incl. Keto Diet and Low Carb Recipes

Bettany Addington

ISBN- 9798620972081

TABLE OF CONTENTS

Slow cooker

Back in the days the cherish dream of every housewife was magical cooking pot that cooks food by itself. Everybody wants to spend less time on the kitchen. Isn't it? It's better of course to make time for your nearest and dearest and at the end of the day for your beloved ones. For the time being there is a smart solution of this problem – slow cooker. This wonderful device is popular already in many families. However, some people are afraid to buy this kitchen utensil because don't know how to use it properly.

So what is slow cooker? Slow cooker is a multifunctional kitchen appliance that has program software and serves for cooking different kinds of meals in automatic mode. In other words while you hanging loose the slow cooker is preparing food.

As you see it is an integral assistant in your kitchen because it significantly simplifies and accelerates food cooking process. To place in a cooking pot necessary ingredients and spices, set proper mode according to your recipe, press several buttons and receive after a while a delicious flavor meal-what can be simpler?

Electric slow cookers are very easy-to-manage gadgets that,with all this simplicity, save up a decent amount of effort and time for their owners. Such a gadget can successfully replace many kitchen appliances, which is especially relevant in the presence of a small living space. When every piece of free space is important in the kitchen, a device that can handle with lots of functions of the stove, oven, bread maker, steamer, deep fryer, yogurt maker and even fondue is a real salvation. The superhero among the kitchen gadgets!

This cookware can be used for cooking,frying, stewing, preheating and steaming. It can prepare extremely delicious cereals and pasta, baking, cooking useful dairy products, baking bread and boiling a thick jam. It's like a little chef in your kitchen that can cope with any meal. A true cyber assistant for the modern hostess!

How to choose a slow cooker and what should I have pay attention to?

A family, looking for such device, should take into consideration their own needs in order to make their purchase successful and handy for a long time.

Selection criteria of the slow cooker

- Presence of **non-stick surface**. If it is present in your model then you won't need to stir the meal every 5 minute and easily wash the device after using. The most expensive slow cookers have five-layered surface with additional marble spraying.

- **Volume.** It's worth taking into account the amount of members in your family: 3L container will be suitable for small families; 5-6L is suitable for big ones.

- The control may be **manual and automatic.** Expensive models have an automatic panel on account which, the chef saves his time up. However, slow cookers with a small set of functions are better to choose with manual controls, as there is no point in overpaying.

- **Quantity and variety of functions.** As a rule, a device accomplishes 6 standard functions, but there exist also devices that have 10 sundry modes.

- It is quite easy to choose the program you need. For baking, there is a mode of "Baking", "Steaming" will allow you to cook healthy recipes for your diet, there are also programs "Steam", "Maintaining heat" and others.

- **A multi-mode timer** is not present in every model. It gives you an opportunity to set the timer beforehand and put off the operation for a while.

- **Power.** Usually, the instructions for slow cookers indicate the maximum potential value. The higher it is, the faster meals are prepared. The best option is a device with a power of 670WT.

- **Security level.** It is especially critical if you have small children. The cooker must be provided with a sealed valve and a soft steam release system. A model with a fixed cord rather than a detachable one will be safer.

- **Economy mode** allows reducing the amount of electricity by 25%.

- **Ergonomics.** This criterion is purely individual so rely on.

Advantages of having a slow cooker

As it was already mentioned the main benefit of a slow cooker is its multifunctionality. This device handles with the preparation of different meals, without requiring the supervision of the owner. In addition, this gadget is able to replace several types of appliances, thus saving both money and free space in the kitchen. But what are other pros of the slow cooker?

✔ Slow cooker's modes allow sticking thoroughly to provide temperature level of the recipe you chose and food cooking duration which is particularly important for healthy recipes and dairy products.

✔ The food is prepared as soon as possible, it isn't overcooked and thanks to it all useful properties and vitamins are preserved.

✔ It is safe to cook in a slow cooker- the temperature and pressure inside the bowl are controlled by special sensors, so the permissible markings are never exceeded. The food is not subjected to excessive heat treatment, and there is no risk of any unpredictable situations when using a slow cooker.

How to look after the slow cooker?

It is quite clear that such device needs a special and thorough care which may be simpler than may seem at a first glance.

So what do you have to know about how to take care of the slow cooker?

1) After each using of the slow cooker bowl, smart valve and steam container must be thoroughly washed and dried. Do it shipshape not to damage non-stick surface.

2) The moisture accumulator needs also to be cleaned from now and then.

3) A special attention should be paid to the lid It has a tendency to adhere all food and fat remains. Remove them when the lid becomes dirty.

4) It is recommended to wash slow cooker bowl without using abrasives and too hard sponges. Despite the coating material (ceramics or Teflon), rough wiping and washing of the bowl can damage the non-stick coating and negate the efforts of many slow cooker functions. It is better to use soft sponges, napkins and ideally- microfiber.

5) Avoid using cleaning powder agents, to save the slow cooker bowl's surface from scrapes. Cleaning gels are more effective and rational. After a careful washing, the slow cooker bowl should be wiped and thoroughly dried - this is important.

6) If you detect a nasty smell in a bowl, you should pour some water add a little of lemon juice. Some people use ginger instead of lemon. It removes bad smell and the slow cooker will be fresh and clean again.

7) It is especially important to pay attention to the care of the exhaust valve – where frequently fatty fumes congestions are happened. What's more it can adversely influence on many manufacturing processes inside a slow cooker during operation.

8) And the last one. Do not forget to monitor the cleanness of the surface where the slow cooker is located, because the cleaner it is, the less likely that garbage from the table or wall will get into the slow cooker itself.

Slow cooker recipes

Approximately the morning of every person starts with a cup of coffee, tea or a glass of juice with delicious meal for breakfast. If you have an opportunity to wind down on holidays and allow yourself to cook something tasty, during working lives-you cannot allow such luxury. Nevertheless, you want to receive something tasty and nutritious in a short time. Then slow cooker comes to your rescue.

Modern kitchen technology allows creating culinary masterpieces without taking pains.

So which recipes are perfectly suitable for slow cooker? Basically you have no restrictions because up-to-date models ensure different functions. It is particularly topical for people who prefer proper nutritious and healthy recipes. Dishes prepared in a slow cooker are more healthy and useful.

So check out the recipes and enjoy your meal!

BREAKFAST

Cottage cheese casserole

Preparation time- 1 hour
Servings- 8
Kcal- 225

Net carbs: 18 /0.63 oz / Fats: 7g / 0.24oz / Proteins: 14 g / 0.49 oz

Ingredients:

- 4eggs
- ¾ cup / 170g sugar
- 2 cups / 500g cottage cheese
- 1 cup / 245g plain yogurt
- ½ cup / 100g semolina
- 1tsp./ 4ml vanilla extract
- 1tsp. / 4g baking powder
- 1/4tsp. / 3g Salt
- Raisins to taste
- Orange / lemon zest

Preparation steps:

1. Whisk eggs during 2-3 minutes until white fluffy mass. Add sugar and beat again. Then add cottage cheese, yogurt, semolina, vanilla, salt and baking powder. In the end add raisins and stir properly. The batter is quite liquid.
2. Lubricate the slow cooker insert bowl with butter. Pour the batter in a bowl. Set «Baking» mode and cook for 45 minutes. If you have a small container then divide the batter into 2 parts and cook 2 casseroles or you can cook one but add extra 20-30 minutes.
3. Serve with honey/favorite jam and mint leaves.

Pancakes

Preparation time- 20minutes
Servings- 8
Kcal-198

Net carbs : 32/ 1.12oz / Fats : 6g / 0.21oz/ Proteins: 6 g/ 0.21oz/

Ingredients:

- 3eggs
- 2 cups / 400ml milk
- 1 cup / 200 ml water
- 3tbsp. / 40g sugar
- Salt
- 2 cups/ 270g flour
- 2 tbsp. / 30ml vegetable oil

Preparation steps:

1. Beat the eggs with salt and sugar. Add flour, mix.
2. Pour in milk and water. Add melted butter, mix again.
3. Turn on the «Baking» mode and let the slow cooker warm up for 5-7 minutes.
4. Using a silicone brush grease the slow cooker bowl with oil.
5. Pour pancake dough with a thin layer on the bottom of the heated bowl.
6. Bake pancake for about 2-3 minutes without closing the slow cooker. Then gently turn over and fry on the opposite side.
7. Reiterate with the rest of the batter.
8. Stuff with favorite filling.

Cereal

Preparation time- 45 minutes
Servings-2
Kcal 184

Net carbs: 24g / 0.84 oz / Fats: 13g / 0.45 oz / Proteins: 8 g / 0.28 oz/

Ingredients:

- 1.5 cup / 300ml Milk
- 2/3 cup / 100g Oatmeal flakes
- Salt
- 1 Apple
- 1/3 cup / 50g Raisins
- 1tbsp. / 15g butter
- 1tbsp. /25g Sugar

Preparation steps:

1. Place oatmeal, salt in a slow cooker. Add sugar or honey.
2. Pour milk and stir well.
3. Close the lid of the slow cooker and press the "Porridge" or "Milk Porridge" mode. Cook for about 12 minutes or according to the set mode.
4. Serve with caramelized apples and raisins.

Cabbage casserole with carrot

Preparation time- 2 hours
Servings-6
Kcal 219

Net carbs: 29 / 1.02oz / Fats: 9g / 0.31oz / Proteins: 9g / 0.31 oz

Ingredients:

- 2 cups / 500 g spinach
- 1 zucchini
- 1 large potato
- 2 carrots
- 4 green chives
- 3 cloves of garlic
- pinch of ground turmeric
- 3 eggs
- 3 tbsp. / 60g flour
- 5 sprigs of dill
- 6 tbsp. / 90ml olive oil
- Black pepper, salt

Preparation steps:

1. Lubricate the slow cooker with olive oil.
2. Rinse vegetables and herbs. Peel potatoes, carrots and zucchini, grate on a coarse grater. Squeeze out excess fluid. Finely chop green onion, dill and garlic, mix with grated vegetables. Cut the spinach into strips. Add to the vegetable mixture. Season with salt, pepper and turmeric.
3. Pour enough flour into the vegetables to make a thick batter. Beat eggs and combine with the mixture.
4. Cook in the "Baking" mode during 45 minutes.

Omelet with vegetables

Preparation time 30 minutes
Servings-6
Kcal 197

Net carbs: 12 / 0.42 oz / Fats: 8g / 0.28 oz / Proteins: 9 g / 0.31 oz

Ingredients:

- 5 eggs
- 1 cup / 200 ml milk
- 1 1/3 cup / 210 g pea
- 2 tomatoes
- 1 cup / 100g grated cheese
- 1 onion
- 2tbsp. / 30 ml olive oil

Preparation steps:

1. Chop the onion, tomatoes. Grate cheese.
2. Pour the olive oil in a slow cooker bowl. Set «Baking» mode. Fry onion for 5 minutes. Then add tomatoes, stir with onion and stew for 5 minutes. Then add pea and combine.
3. Beat eggs, add salt and pepper. Add milk and keep on whisking.
4. Add vegetable to eggs' mixture. Strew with cheese. Cover and cook for 20 minutes.
5. Serve with spinach and parsley.

Pumpkin porridge

Preparation time 35 minutes
Servings-5
Kcal 100

Net carbs: 17 / 0.59oz /Fats: 4g / 0.14oz/ Proteins: 3g/ 0.10oz/

Ingredients:

- 2 cups / 500 g pumpkin
- ¾ cup / 150 g rice
- 1 ¼ cup / 300ml milk
- 2/3 cup / 150 ml water
- 1/3 cup / 70g butter
- ¾ cup / 150g sugar/honey
- Salt.

Preparation steps:

1. Rinse the pumpkin and peel. Cut into cubes and tranfer in a slow cooker.
2. Pour water inside, add butter and cover with a lid. Set «Baking» mode for 25 minutes. If you prefer the consistence like pudding then after cooking puree the pumpkin.
3. Wash the rice thoroughly in cold water. After 25 minutes of cooking, add rice, sugar and salt. Pour all milk and set «Porridge» mode if you don't have this one then «Stewing». Set 30-50 minutes. It depends on your slow cooker.
4. To make the taste more saturated you may add cinnamon, nutmeg. Also you may add dried fruits but then it will be more caloric.

Rice casserole with cottage cheese and apples

Preparation time 1 hour
Servings-5
Kcal 169

Net carbs: 19 / 0.67oz / Fats:5 g /0.17 oz / Proteins:10 g / 0.35 oz

Ingredients:

- 1 cup / 180g boiled rice
- 2 apples
- 3 tbsp./ 45g sugar
- 1 1/3 cup/ 300g cottage cheese
- 1 carrot
- 2 eggs
- Cinnamon / vanilla
- Raisins, dried fruits optional

Preparation steps:

1. Boil rice to softness. Combine rice, cottage cheese, sugar, eggs and cinnamon. Add peeled and diced apples. Mix thoroughly. Add grated carrot and dried fruits.
2. Grease slow cooker bowl with butter.
3. Place ready mixture in a slow cooker bowl and level it. Cook in «Baking» mode for 30-40 minutes.
4. Cool the ready casserole firstly in a slow cooker and then out of it.
5. Serve with fruits and honey.

Cottage cheese pancakes

Preparation time 25 minutes
Servings-4
Kcal 200

Net carbs: 19g / 0.67oz / Fats:8g / 0.28 oz / Proteins: 15g / 0.52 oz

Ingredients:

- 2 cups / 410g cottage cheese
- 2eggs
- 2-3tbsp. / 35g sugar
- 2tbsp. / flour
- Vanilla extract
- Coconut oil (for frying)

Preparation steps:

1. Rub cheese through metal sieve. When the consistency is homogeneous add sugar or you can replace sugar with sugar powder if you want. Add eggs of room temperature, vanilla extract. Mix everything thoroughly.
2. Add sift flour. Mix well again. Don't add too much flour in order to make cottage cheese pancakes soft and tender.
3. Add 1 tsp. of coconut oil in a slow cooker bowl. Turn the mode «Baking».
4. Make small balls from cheese dough. Press each ball, forming flat cheesecakes. Fry the cheesecakes with the lid closed for 3-4 minutes on either side.
5. Let cool. Sprinkle ready pancakes with sugar powder or serve with honey or jam to your taste.
6. P.S. You may also add dried fruits, coconut flakes or chocolate for stuffing pancakes according to your taste.

Shakshuka

Preparation time 30 minutes
Servings-4
Kcal: 120

Net carbs: 5 / 0.17 oz / Fats:8 g / 0.28 oz / Proteins: 6g / 0.21oz

Ingredients:

- 1 cup / 210g canned tomatoes
- 2 red bell peppers
- 2eggs
- 1 onion
- 1 garlic clove
- Cheese (optional)
- Mixed spices (pepper, parsley, salt, turmeric, mint, nutmeg)

Preparation steps:

1. Firstly, cut the sweet pepper and chili in half, remove the seeds. Then cut the flesh into cubes. Chop finely the onion and garlic. Pour olive oil into the slow cooker bowl; switch on the «Frying» mode. Add turmeric and warm up. Add onion and pepper. Cook additional 10 minutes, stirring from now and then.

2. Add canned tomatoes, chopped parsley. Proceed cooking for about 10 minutes. Carefully, trying not to damage the yolks, break the eggs and add them into the prepared vegetables. Season with salt. Cook for about 5 minutes.

3. Sprinkle with mint leaves before serving.

Stuffed peppers

Preparation time 1 hour
Servings-8
Kcal : 156

Net carbs: 6g / 0.21 oz / Fats: 9g / 0.31 oz / Proteins: 10g / 0.36 oz

- 2 cups / 400g minced beef
- ½ cup /100g rice
- 1 cup /200g tomato sauce
- 1 onion
- 1 cup / 200g sour cream
- 8 red bell peppers
- Salt, pepper
- Parsley chopped
- Olive oil

Preparation steps:

1. Firstly put rice in a slow cooker dish, pour 1 glass of water and cook using «Porridge» mode for 40 minutes. Then add olive oil. Set «Frying» mode. Throw in chopped onion and keep on cooking for 10 minutes.
2. Mix In a separate bowl onion, minced beef, rice and chopped parsley. Dust with salt and ground pepper.
3. Prepare peppers. Cut off the top and scoop out seeds. Stuff with filling and transfer peppers in a slow cooker.
4. Turn «Multicook» mode, set 120 °C / 248 °F and cook for 35-40 minutes. Add sour cream and tomato sauce to peppers, season with salt somewhat. Go on cooking for 25 minutes.
5. Serve with favorite sauce and chopped dill.

MAIN DISH

Meat Recipes

Musaka

Preparation time 1.30 hour
Servings-6
Kcal: 150

Net carbs: 9g / 0.31 oz / Fats: 10g / 0.35 oz / Proteins: 6g / 0.21oz

Ingredients:

For topping

- 2.5lbs / 1kg lamb mince 0,5 cup / 50g Parmesan cheese
- 3 eggplants 0,5 cup / flour
- 3 tomatoes 1.5 cup /300ml milk
- 2 onion 1 egg
- 2 garlic cloves 2tbsp. / 30g butter
- 4-5 mint leaves parsley
- Spices (coriander, nutmeg, salt, pepper, clove)

Preparation steps:

1. Peel the eggplants and cut into circles. Then season with salt and put aside for 15 minutes. After, wash and dry using paper towels. Roll circles in flour from both sides, leave for 3 minutes. Pour olive oil in a slow cooker bowl, turn «Frying» mode. Fry for 3-4 minutes from each side. Place ready eggplants on a napkin to absorb extra fat.

2. Grate cheese. Chop the parsley. Turn «Multicook» 120 °C / 248 °F mode, for 25 minutes. Melt the butter. Add flour continually stirring 10 minutes. Beat warm milk with eggs in a separate bowl. Add this mixture to slow cooker with flour and stir properly, cook stirring, for about 10 minutes. Add grated Parmesan and greenery. Mix properly and place in a bowl. Put aside. Chop the tomatoes, garlic and onion. Combine mince with vegetables and spices.

3. Grease slow cooker with olive oil. Make Musaka in layers. 1-eggplants, 2-mince, 3-sauce.Repeat. Set «Multicook» mode for 35 minutes 140°C /284°F. Then open a lid and keep on cooking for 15 minutes.

4. Serve with favorite greenery.

Mutton ribs

Preparation time: 2hours
Servings-5
Kcal: 372

Net carbs: 0g / 0oz /Fats: 70g / 2.46 oz / Proteins: 30g /1.05 oz

Ingredients:

- 🍽 3.5lbs / 1.5kg lamb ribs
- 🍽 20g / fresh ginger
- 🍽 2 onions
- 🍽 1 cup / 200ml dry red wine
- 🍽 ½ cup / 50g fresh parsley and cilantro;
- 🍽 1tsp. / 5g thyme
- 🍽 1tsp. / 5g ground pepper black and red
- 🍽 1tsp. / 5g dried mint
- 🍽 4 garlic cloves;
- 🍽 Sea salt

Preparation steps:

1. Cut ribs into equal pieces, wash. Cut the skin and dry the meat with paper towels.
2. Peel the ginger root, finely chop or grate. Free the onion from the husk, chop into quarters, and transfer to a deep container and shake with your hands. Let the onion release its juice for the marinade.
3. Chop fresh greenery. Add greenery, ginger and other spices except salt to onion. Place ribs into marinade mix with hands, and pour with wine. Transfer ribs in the refrigerator for 6-8 hours for marinating. Every 2 hours stir the marinade for equal spices saturation.

4. Set the "Stewing" mode for 90 minutes. Load the mutton with the marinade into the slow cooker bowl.

5. Add the garlic passed through the press, and salt. Combine the ingredients thoroughly. Close the lid and cook until the signal.

6. After the stew is finished, let the meat absorb all spices and flavors turning on the "Warm Up" mode for 15-20 minutes.

7. Serve hot with any side dish.

Pilaf with duck's

Preparation time 1.30 hour
Servings-6
Kcal: 170

Net carbs: 20g / 0.70oz / Fats: 10g / 0.35 oz / Proteins: 7g / 0.24 oz

Ingredients:

- 2lbs / 800 g duck
- 1carrot
- 2onion
- 4 garlic cloves
- 1 ½ cup / 300g long-grain rice
- 4 cups / 800ml water
- 1tbsp. / ready seasoning for pilaf
- Salt.

Preparation steps:

1. Rinse the duck carcass in running water and pat it dry with a paper towel.
2. Switch on the slow cooker and select the "Frying" mode .When the bowl warmed up well, put a little bit of duck fat on the bottom.
3. Dice the onion. Fry it in a duck's fat during 4 minutes. Then add sliced duck and cook in the mode for 15 minutes.
4. Cut carrot into circles and add in the slow cooker. Add salt and all spices. Stir thoroughly. Add chopped garlic and water. Change the mode into «Steaming» Cook for 43 minutes.
5. Wash the rice and drain extra liquid. When the slow cooker finished working add rice in the bowl .Set the mode «Pilaf» 30-35 minutes.
6. You will be pleasantly surprised how delicious, flavor and crumbly will be our pilaf. And everything thanks to our indispensable device!

Pea cream with chicken

Preparation time 1 hour
Servings-4
Kcal: 214

Net carbs: 12 g / 0.42 oz / Fats: 8 g / 0.28oz / Proteins:6 g / 0.21oz

Ingredients:

- 1 cup / 200g split pea
- 1 carrot
- 4 potatoes
- 1 onion
- 0.7lbs / 300g chicken fillet
- 1 processed cheese
- ½ cup / 100 ml cream high fat
- salt, pepper ,dried spices to taste
- Greenery at your discretion.

Preparation steps:

1. Soak peas in cold water in advance for 2-3 hours. Perfectly – for 24 hours.
2. Pour 2 L water in a slow cooker cup, add pea. Turn on «Baking mode» for 20 minutes. (To make water boil faster)Then as soon as it boils switch «Soup» mode and cook for 45 minutes. After boiling, add washed and diced chicken, when the broth is brought to boil, take off the foam.
3. After add chopped potato and after 10 minutes-carrot and onion previously diced. Add spices. Stir well.
4. Cut the processed cheese into cubes. Combine with cream. Place in a food processor. Pulse until homogeneous mass. When the soup is cooked through, add cream mixture and continuously stir. Bring to boil using «Soup» or «Baking» mode.
5. Garnish with crisp toasts and chopped greenery.

Turkey cutlets

Preparation time 50 minutes
Servings-4
Kcal: 230

Net carbs: 9g/ 0.31oz / Fats: 13g / 0.45oz/ Proteins: 19g / 0.67 oz

Ingredients:

- 1.2 lb / 600g Minced meat
- 2 pieces White bread
- ½ cup / 100 ml Milk
- 1 Onion
- 1 Egg
- Salt
- Pepper
- Spices
- Greenery
- Vegetable oil

Preparation steps:

1. To begin with, put sliced white bread in a deep container and pour milk or water pieces of bread swell. Cut the onion into small pieces.

2. If you have prepared meat for cutlets, grind it in a meat grinder together with onions and bread, each piece of which needs to be squeezed out a little to remove the redundant liquid. If you use ready-made meat, then cut the onion into small cubes .After add to the mince, also remove extra liquid from bread and knead with your hands over the meat.

3. Break 2 eggs in a ready mixture, season with salt and pepper, and spices. Knead the mince thoroughly with hands. Form 12 round cutlets. Place in a previously greased with oil slow cooker bowl and turn the «Frying» mode. Fry on each side for 3 minutes.

4. Then switch «Frying» mode off, place all cutlets in a slow cooker, pour 1 cup water, close the slow cooker with a lid and turn on «Stewing» mode for 20 minutes.

5. Serve with spinach.

Fish Recipes

Teriyaki salmon with spinach

Preparation time 35 minutes
Servings-4
Kcal: 280

Net carbs: 5g / 0.17oz / Fats: 17g / 0.59oz / Proteins: 24 g / 0.84 oz

Ingredients:

- 4 salmon fillets
- ½ cup / 115 ml teriyaki sauce
- 2 tbsp. / 30ml rice vinegar
- 2tsp./ 30ml sesame oil
- 2tsp./ 10g fresh ginger root
- 2 garlic cloves
- baby spinach

Preparation steps:

1. Lubricate the slow cooker bowl with oil. Turn on the «Stewing» mode.
2. Put salmon fillets inside. Mix the teriyaki, vinegar, oil, ginger and garlic in a separate bowl. Pour the mixture over the fish. Close the slow cooker and cook in «Stewing» mode for 30 minutes.
3. Serve with spinach the rest of teriyaki sauce.

Fish ragout

Preparation time 30 minutes
Servings-4
Kcal: 230

Net carbs: 0 g/ 0oz / Fats 18g / 0.63oz/ Proteins: 22g / 0.77oz

Ingredients:

- 28oz / 800g fish
- 1-2 red bell pepper
- 3-4 potatoes
- 1-2 zucchini
- 1-2 carrot
- 1 leek
- 1-2 tbsp./ 30g tomato sauce
- Spices
- Olive oil
- 1 cup / 200 ml Vegetable broth

Preparation steps:

1. Wash the fish fillet, pat with paper towel and cut into slices.
2. Slice leek. Chop potatoes, pepper, carrot and zucchini.
3. Turn on the slow cooker. Set the «Frying» mode. Pour oil into the slow cooker bowl and wait for the device to warm up. Then put the leek with carrots and cook for about 8 minutes and without a lid. Switch the «Frying» mode off.
4. Stow the fish in a slow cooker. Add vegetables. Season with spice, salt and peppers. Pour tomato sauce and carefully stir with a wooden spoon. Close the slow cooker with a lid. Turn the «Stewing» mode for 15 minutes. After10 minutes after signal, release the steam, take off the lid and check ragout.
5. Serve with favorite fresh greenery.

Fish cutlets

Preparation time: 40 minutes
Servings-5
Kcal: 140

Net carbs: 8g / 0.28oz / Fats: 9g /0.31 oz / Proteins: 14 g / 0.28 oz

Ingredients:

- 2lbs /400 g minced fish
- 1 large onion
- 3 garlic cloves
- 3 wheat bread slices
- 1 cup / 200ml water
- 1 tbsp. / 26g butter
- salt
- spices to taste

Preparation steps:

1. In a deep bowl combine minced fish, salt and pepper to taste. Peel onion and garlic, chop. Grind in a food processor with minced fish.
2. In a separate bowl soak the bread. Drain extra liquid, somewhat wringing out bread with hands.
3. Break egg in a cup, add a pinch of salt and whisk with fork.
4. With wet hands shape medium sized cutlets, press each cutlet forming round shape. Transfer all cutlets in a previously greased slow cooker bowl. Turn on «Stewing» mode. Add 1 L water and put some butter. Cook 20 minutes. After 10 minutes open the lid, turn cutlets over pour with the rest of the butter, close the lid and cook until signal
5. Serve with any side dish or vegetable salad.

Fish casserole

Preparation time: 30minutes
Servings: 4
Kcal: 140

Net carbs: 8g / 0.28 oz / Fats: 7 g / 0.24 oz / Proteins: 12g / 0.42 oz

Ingredients:

- 2 lbs. / 1 Hake fish
- 15oz / 400 g potato
- 1 onion
- 3tbsp. / 45ml vegetable oil
- Ground pepper, salt
- 1 cup / 100g Parmesan cheese
- 3eggs

Preparation steps:

1. Cut the fish into fillets and then into small pieces. Dust with salt and pepper.
2. Boil jacket potato. Peel and grate. Season with salt and pepper.
3. Turn on the slow cooker and set «Baking» mode. Peel and chop the onion and fry on the vegetable oil.
4. Grease slow cooker bowl with oil. Spread grated potato combined with onion on the bottom and level it. Then put fish layer.
5. Combine eggs with grated cheese. Pour it over the fish. Cook in «Baking» mode for about 30 minutes. Let cool.
6. Serve with spinach.

Salmon soup

Preparation time: 1 hour
Servings: 6
Kcal: 156

Net carbs: 25g / 0.88oz / Fats: 9g / 0.31oz/ Proteins: 25 g / 0.88 oz

Ingredients:

- 1 Salmon
- 3 Potato
- 1 Onion
- 1 Carrot
- ½ cup / 100g rice

- 1 cup / 2 L Water
- Salt
- Spices
- Greenery

Preparation steps:

1. Clean, wash, remove gills of fish. Put the fish in the slow cooker bowl.
2. Dice potatoes. Chop the carrots into cubes. Rinse rice.
3. Add potatoes, carrots, rice, and onion to the slow cooker to the fish. Add water, salt, spices
4. Set the slow cooker to the "Stewing" mode for 1 hour (if you use hot water to cook fish soup in a slow cooker, it will take much less time). The degree of readiness of fish soup in the slow cooker can be determined by the readiness of the potato.

Seafood recipes

Prawns in a butter-garlic sauce

Preparation time: 20 minutes
Servings: 2
Kcal: 150

Net carbs: 2g / 0.07 oz / Fats: 7 g / 0.24oz/ Proteins: 16g / 0.56oz

Ingredients:

- 🍽 17oz / 500 g prawns
- 🍽 1 onion
- 🍽 2 garlic cloves

- 🍽 ¼ cup / 55g butter
- 🍽 1 basil sprig
- 🍽 Salt, pepper

For the sauce

- 🍽 2 cups / 500 ml cream
- 🍽 1 cup / 100g Cheese

- 🍽 1 1/8 cup/ 250g tomato sauce

Preparation steps:

1. Chop garlic, onion and basil. Grate the cheese.
2. Remove the shell from the prawns.
3. Place the butter, garlic, onion and shrimps in a slow cooker bowl. Turn the baking mode and cook for about 20 minutes.
4. In a separate bowl combine cream, tomato sauce and cheese.
5. After 10 minutes of cooking, open the lid of a slow cooker and sprinkle the meal with basil, add salt and pepper to taste. Stir properly. Pour the cream sauce, stir thoroughly. Cover and cook to the end of mode.
6. Serve as a main course and garnish with chopped greenery.

Paella with seafood

Preparation time: 40 minutes
Servings: 4
Kcal: 140

Net carbs: 17 g / 0.59 oz / Fats: 4 g /0.14 oz/ Proteins: 8 g /0.28 oz

Ingredients:

- 🍴 16oz / 450g king prawns
- 🍴 9 oz / 250g mussels
- 🍴 5 squids
- 🍴 3 tomatoes
- 🍴 5 garlic cloves
- 🍴 2 red bell pepper
- 🍴 2 ¼ cup / 500g long-grain rice
- 🍴 4tbsp. / 90ml olive oil
- 🍴 2/3 cup / 155ml dry white wine
- 🍴 3 cups / 600ml water or vegetable broth.
- 🍴 1tsp. / 7g mixture of Italian herbs
- 🍴 salt, pepper to taste;

Preparation steps:

1. Thaw out squids. Boil in salty water. After water starts boiling, cook for 3-4 minutes. Thaw out mussels diving each of them in the boiling water. Then rinse thoroughly. Thaw out shrimps, and remove the shell.
2. Set the slow cooker in «Frying» mode , pour in 2 tablespoons of olive oil.
3. Peel the garlic, chop it with a knife and put to a slow cooker.

4. When the oil absorbs the scent of garlic, take out this ingredient. Add mussels and shrimps in hot oil flavored with garlic. Fry for 2-3 minutes.

5. Lightly salt the mussels and shrimps, add pepper and pour dry white wine into the slow cooker. Continue frying until the wine is evaporated (5-6 minutes).

6. Cut squids into rings. Transfer them to the slow cooker with previously roasted garlic. Carry on frying for 2 minutes.

7. Wash the pepper, free it from seeds and pedicels. Cut the vegetable into strips.

8. Rinse the tomatoes, scald with boiling water and take off the skin. Cut the vegetables into small cubes.

9. Peel the onion, chop it into small cubes with a knife. Place vegetables to seafood.

10. Set the slow cooker again in frying mode,add another 2 tbsp. of olive oil.

11. Fry the contents of the slow cooker for 3-5 minutes, add salt at the end of this step.

12. Rinse rice under a plentiful stream of cold water.

13. Transfer rice to the slow cooker, fry until translucent.

14. Pour the contents of the appliance with water, add a mixture of Italian herbs, salt and pepper.

15. Set the slow cooker in the" pilaf" mode; prepare the dish - 40 minutes.

16. Serve with vegetable salad and crunchy toasts.

Spaghetti with shrimps in creamy sauce

Preparation time: 30 minutes
Servings: 3
Kcal: 290

Net carbs: 19g / 0.67 oz / Fats: 19 g / 0.67oz/ Proteins: 11g / 0.38 oz

Ingredients:

- 3 cups / 300g spaghetti
- 11oz / 300g boiled peeled shrimps
- 1 garlic clove
- 2tbsp. / 30ml vegetable oil
- 1tbsp. / 15ml lemon juice
- 1 cup / 200 ml cream 25%
- 4 sprigs dill
- 4 sprigs parsley

Preparation steps:

1. Boil spaghetti to softness. Drop in a colander, cover. Put aside in a warm place.
2. Peel and chop the garlic. Turn the mode «Multicook» by 160 °C / 320°F, heat up the oil and fry the garlic for 30 seconds. Add shrimps, splash with lemon juice, pour cream mix thoroughly and boil the sauce until thickened, 5 min.
3. Add spaghetti, stir well and after 5 minutes serve in plates with freshly chopped parsley and dill.

Prawns cutlets with corn

Preparation time: 1.45 minutes
Servings: 4
Kcal: 193

Net carbs: 5 g / 0.17 oz / Fats: 16 g / 0.56oz/ Proteins: 7 g / 0.24oz

Ingredients:

- 7oz / 200g peeled prawns
- 1 cup / 200g freshly frozen corn grains
- 35oz / 1kg jacket potato
- 1 bunch chives
- 2 sprigs parsley
- 2tbsp. / 20g flour
- 2 tbsp./ 30g butter
- Salt, pepper

Preparation steps:

1. Grate potato. Rinse the onion and parsley, dry and chop. Thaw out the corn. Add chopped greenery, corn and shrimps to potato. Season with salt and pepper, stirring thoroughly.
2. Divide obtained mass into 8 parts and make 8 round cutlets. Place them on a wooden board and put in a fridge for 1 hour.
3. Place cutlets in a slow cooker, close the lid, turn on «Steaming» mode and cook for about 20 minutes.
4. Serve with slices of lemon.

Scallops with pasta

Preparation time: 30 minutes
Servings: 3
Kcal: 340

Net carbs: 71 g / 2.5 oz / Fats: 2g / 0.07 oz/ Proteins: 12 g / 0.42 oz

Ingredients:

- 3 cups / 300g pasta
- 7oz / 200g canned mushrooms
- 1 onion
- 7 oz / 200g scallops
- 1 cup / 200 g fat cream
- Spices, chopped greenery, salt
- Parmesan

Preparation steps:

1. Rinse scallops under running cold water and boil for some minutes.
2. Boil pasta in salty water. While pasta is being prepared, peel the onion and chop it.
3. Cut mushrooms. Turn «Frying» mode, pour some sunflower oil, add onion and fry until soft. Add canned mushrooms and keep on cooking. After add scallops and pour cream, let it steam until cream is thick.
4. Sieve cooked pasta through colander and transfer them into a slow cooker. Stir well.
5. Serve with grated Parmesan.

Vegetarian/Vegan/Vegetables

Lentil soup with eggplant

Preparation time: 1.30 minutes
Servings:
Kcal: 60

Net carbs: 6g / 0.21oz / Fats: 4g / 0.14 oz/ Proteins: 3g / 0.10 oz

Ingredients:

- 1 Eggplant
- 1 Carrots
- ½ cup / 100g Red lentils
- 1L water
- 2 Potatoes

- 1 Tomatoes
- paprika, coriander, bay leaf
- 4tbsp/ 90ml Vegetable oil
- Salt to taste

Preparation steps:

1. Rinse and soak lentils overnight or for a couple of hours. Peel potatoes and carrots. Cut potatoes into cubes. Rub carrots on a coarse grater. Cut eggplant into pieces larger than potatoes. Slightly cut the tomatoes, pour over boiling water, then with cold water and peel off. Chop the tomatoes finely.

2. Pour oil in a slow cooker cup, throw in onion, and fry for about 4 minutes in a «Frying» mode. Add carrot and fry for more 3 minutes. After add diced tomatoes, eggplant, potatoes and lentil. Cook for 5 minutes. Season with salt and pepper. Pour with boiling water and cook in a «Soup» mode until it boils. After change the mode into «Stewing» mode and cook for 1.30 minutes.

3. Serve with chopped greenery and crunchy toasts.

Curry rice

Preparation time: 55minutes
Servings: 5
Kcal: 160

Net carbs: 25g / 0.88 oz / Fats: 6 g / 0.21oz/ Proteins: 3g /0.10 oz

Ingredients:

- ½ cup / 100g Long grain rice
- 1.2 cup / 250ml water
- 1 onion
- 2 garlic cloves
- 25g / 1.5tbsp butter
- 1.5tsp./ 8g curry powder
- 2tbsp./ 30ml olive oil
- Salt, pepper

Preparation steps:

1. Grate carrot. Chop onion and garlic. Turn on the «Frying» or «Baking» mode. Quickly pour the olive oil and put a piece of butter. After the butter melts, pour the garlic and, stirring constantly, for 30 seconds, fry it in oil.
2. After add onion and curry powder. Then add carrot. Keep on frying for about 3 minutes.
3. Combine the rice with other the ingredients so that the whole rice is coated with oil. Pour boiling water, salt, bring to a boil, mix and close the lid. Cook in the "Stewing" mode for 20 minutes. Then switch off the slow cooker and let the rice brew for another 15 minutes. Only then lid may be opened.
4. Serve with lettuce.

Couscous

Preparation time: 30 minutes
Servings: 4
Kcal: 345

Net carbs: 72g / 2.53 oz / Fats: 2 g / 0.07 oz/ Proteins: 13g / 0.45 oz

Ingredients:

- 🍽 1 eggplant
- 🍽 1 tomato
- 🍽 Olive oil
- 🍽 1 bell pepper

- 🍽 1cup / 200g couscous
- 🍽 2 cups / 400ml water
- 🍽 Salt, pepper

Preparation steps:

1. Wash and cut eggplant, pepper and tomato. Add onion and garlic (optional).
2. Pour olive oil in a slow cooker, add chopped eggplant, and set «Baking» mode for 40 minutes.
3. Fry until soft, add tomatoes and pepper. Season with salt and ground pepper, mix thoroughly. Fry everything together. Add couscous and pour with boiling water. The quantity of water may vary depending on couscous kind. Cook for 7-10 minutes. Let it stay in a slow cooker for 10 minutes before turning it off. The couscous will absorb all vegetable flavors and will be crumbly.
4. Serve with your favorite greenery.

Curry with chickpeas, tofu and coconut milk

Preparation time: 40 minutes
Servings: 4
Kcal: 156

Net carbs: 16g / 0.56oz / Fats: 6 g / 0.21oz / Proteins: 8g / 0.28 oz

Ingredients:

- 🍽 1 cup / 200g chickpeas
- 🍽 1 cup / 250ml coconut milk
- 🍽 7oz / 200g canned tomatoes
- 🍽 3 garlic cloves
- 🍽 1 onion

- 🍽 5oz / 150g tofu
- 🍽 1tsp./ 3g curry powder
- 🍽 3tbsp./ 35ml lime juice
- 🍽 Coconut oil
- 🍽 Spices to taste

Preparation steps:

1. Soak chickpeas in water for 4 hours in advance. Put the chickpeas in a pan, pour water and cook in a «Porridge» mode for 40 minutes-1 hour.
2. Chop onion and garlic in small pieces.
3. Turn on «Frying» mode and let the slow cooker warm up well . Pour vegetable oil. Add in chili flakes, garlic and onions.
4. Fry until the onions and garlic become translucent and a bright aroma appears.
5. Add spices and fry for more than 1 minute stirring. Pour coconut milk and tomato pieces together with juice. Season with salt. Cook for more than 7 minutes until it is thick. Add boiled chickpeas and tofu pieces. Warm up.
6. Dress with lime juice and stir well.
7. Serve with chopped parsley.

Vegan chocolate

Preparation time: 20 minutes
Servings:
Kcal: 800

Net carbs: 4g / 0.14oz / Fats: 52 g / 1.83 oz / Proteins: 4g / 0.14 oz

Ingredients:

- 🍽 3tbsp./ 25g carob
- 🍽 ½ tbsp./ 2g Cinnamon
- 🍽 1 cup / 200ml Coconut oil

- 🍽 1/4tsp. / 3g pinch pink salt
- 🍽 Stuffing 5 tbsp. (sunflower seeds or nuts, dried fruits, such as raisins.)

Preparation steps:

1. Heat the oil in a water bath (water boils in a saucepan, and from the top there is a metal enameled bowl and it heats up).
2. Add carob, cinnamon, and a pinch of salt to it. Mix lumps until smooth.
3. Add to taste the seeds / raisins / nuts (pre-soaked overnight and washed).
4. Mix everything, let it cool slightly and pour it into silicone molds, put it in the refrigerator for a couple of hours, and preferably at night.

Bulgur with vegetables

Preparation time: 30 minutes
Servings: 2
Kcal: 129

Net carbs: 17g / 0.59oz / Fats: 4g / 0.14 oz/ Proteins: 5g / 0.17 oz

Ingredients:

- ½ cup / 100g bulgur
- 1 cup / 200ml water
- 1 onion
- 1 bell pepper
- 1 carrot
- Olive oil
- Salt, pepper
- Greenery

Preparation steps:

1. Rinse and peel vegetables. Scoop out seeds from the pepper.
2. Chop the onion. Grate carrot. Dice pepper.
3. Pour olive oil in a slow cooker bowl. Turn «Frying» or «Baking» mode.
4. Place vegetables in a slow cooker and cook with open lid for about 15 minutes periodically stirring.
5. Rinse bulgur under running water, until water is clear.
6. Pour a glass of water into the slow cooker bowl and wait until water boils. Turn off the program "Frying" and turn on the program "Porridge" or "Buckwheat". Pour bulgur into the slow cooker bowl. Add salt to taste. Mix. Close the lid of the slow cooker and cook for 20-25 minutes.
7. Ready bulgur absorbs all the water and grows in size.
8. Serve with greenery.

Croquette with vegetables

Preparation time: 30 minutes
Servings: 8
Kcal: 193

Net carbs: 7g / 0.24 oz / Fats: 15 g / 0.52 oz/ Proteins: 8g / 0.28 oz

Ingredients:

- 1 lb / 0.5 kg minced beef
- 2 carrots
- 1 pepper
- 1 egg
- 2 onion
- Salt
- 2 cup water
- 1/2 cup / 100g rice
- Paprika to taste
- 1,5 tbsp. / 20g butter
- 1 tbsp. / 15g tomato paste
- 2 tbsp. / 30g sour cream

Preparation steps:

1. Grind meat. In a big bowl mix minced beef, egg, rice, grated carrot, chopped onion. Add salt and paprika.
2. Make croquets.
3. Turn on the slow cooker, set the «Frying» mode, melt butter in a bowl, put meatballs in a slow cooker and fry for 10 minutes on both sides. It is necessary so that meatballs keep their shape during the cooking process.

4. Chop the onion, grate the carrots on a coarse grater, and chop the bell pepper in small pieces. After the slow cooker gave a signal about the end of the Frying mode, reset the mode and cover the vegetables with meatballs.

5. In one glass of hot water, dilute sour cream, in the second glass, dilute tomato paste and carefully pour our meatballs.

6. Close the slow cooker and set the «Stewing» mode (40 minutes).

7. Serve with sliced tomatoes.

Vegan bread

Preparation time: 40 minutes
Servings: 1
Kcal: 210

Net carbs: 33g / 1.16 oz / Fats: 6 g / 0.21 oz/ Proteins: 8g / 0.28 oz

Ingredients:

- 1/2 cup / 65g wheat flour
- ½ cup / 55g instant oat flakes
- 1/2 cup / 65g flour
- 3tbsp./ 50g butter
- 1tbsp. / 25g sugar
- 1tsp. / 6g salt
- 2tsp. / 12g soda
- 2tbsp./ 50g wheat brans
- 1 cup / 250g kefir

Preparation steps:

1. Melt the butter. In a big bowl mix kefir and butter. Add 2 kinds of flour, oat flakes, brans, baking soda, salt and sugar.

2. Mix thoroughly permanently kneading dough. Grease the slow cooker with butter. Place ready bread ball in a slow cooker bowl. Close the lid; turn on «Baking» mode for about 30 minutes.

3. Take out bread from the slow cooker our ready bread, cover with towel and leave for 30 minutes to cool.

Cabbage casserole with potato

Preparation time: 1.30minutes
Servings: 6
Kcal: 122

Net carbs: 8g / 0.28oz / Fats: 6g / 0.21oz / Proteins: 5g / 0.17 oz

Ingredients:

- 5 potatoes
- 18 oz / 500g mushrooms
- 1 carrot
- 2 eggs
- 2 onion
- Salt, pepper
- Sunflower oil
- Sour

Preparation steps:

1. Peel onion and cut into rings, chop mushrooms. Fry mushrooms and onion on sunflower oil.
2. Peel carrot and potato, grate.
3. Mix potato, carrot, and fried mushrooms with vegetables. Add eggs salt pepper and mix properly.
4. Grease the bowl of the slow cooker with vegetable oil, put the prepared mass there and lightly tamp.
5. Cook in the «Baking» mode for 60-80 minutes. Leave the cooked casserole in a cup for 20-30 minutes, and then remove, turn the bowl over on a set plate.
6. Serve with sour cream.

Carrot cutlets

Preparation time: 25 minutes
Servings: 6
Kcal: 40

Net carbs: 9g / 0.31 oz / Fats: 0 g / 0oz / Proteins: 5g / 0.17 oz

Ingredients:

- 3 carrots
- 2 eggs
- 4tbsp./ 100g semolina
- Salt, pepper

Preparation steps:

1. Grate carrot or liquidize in a food processor.
2. Add semolina, eggs, salt and pepper.
3. Mix everything and leave for 20 minutes., In the meantime, semolina should swell.
4. Pour boiling water into slow cooker bowl, set Steaming mode. Blind the patties and put them in the pan. Cook on steam for 25 minutes.
5. Delicious and healthy carrot steam cutlets are ready!

Soup, Stews, Chills

Chili

Preparation time: 6 hours
Servings: 6

Kcal:

Net carbs: 9g / 0.31 oz / Fats: 2g / 0.07oz / Proteins: 3g / 0.10oz

Ingredients:

- 28oz / 800g tomatoes
- 4 cup / 800ml vegetable broth
- 14oz / 400g canned red beans
- 1 cup / 150g chopped onion
- 14oz / 400g canned black beans
- 1 green bell pepper
- 1 cup / 150g frozen green beans
- 2 chopped garlic cloves
- 1 tbsp. / 7g l chopped jalapeno pickled peppers
- 2 tbsp. /`16g dried oregano
- 2tbsp. / 16g chili powder
- 1/3 tbsp. / 9g chopped fresh cilantro leaves
- 2 tsp. /14g ground cumin
- 1 - 2 tsp. / 15ml hot sauce
- 1 tsp. /4g ground coriander
- 1/3 tbsp. / 2g couscous
- 1/2 tbsp. / 50g grated cheese
- Salt and freshly ground black pepper

Preparation steps:

1. Combine all the ingredients except couscous, grated cheese, cilantro, salt and pepper in a slow cooker.
2. Close the lid and cook in the "LOW" mode for 6 - 8 hours or in the "HIGH" mode for 3 - 4 hours. 5 to 10 minutes before the end of cooking (depending on the selected mode) add couscous, close the lid and cook until the couscous is soft.
3. Season the dish to taste with salt and black pepper. Before serving, sprinkle each serving with grated cheese and cilantro.

Soup with meatballs

Preparation time: 40 minutes
Servings: 8
Kcal: 159

Net carbs: 12g / 0.42 oz / Fats: 10g / 0.35oz / Proteins: 5g /0.17 oz

Ingredients:

- 10oz / 300g Minced beef
- 1 onion
- 1 carrot
- 4 potatoes
- 25g vermicelli.
- 1/3 cup 40g dill
- Salt, pepper
- Vegetable oil

Preparation steps:

1. Pour vegetable oil into the slow cooker bowl and turn on the "Frying" mode. Chop onions, grate carrots on a coarse grater. Fry vegetables in oil until golden. Turn off the "Frying" mode.

2. Wash, peel and dice potatoes. Add to onions and carrots and mix everything thoroughly. If you decide to do without frying vegetables, then prepared vegetables – onions, carrots, potatoes, put in a slow cooker bowl.

3. Pour vegetables with 1.5 liters of hot water. Close the lid and turn on the "Soup" mode for 20 minutes.

4. With wet hands roll round meatballs of equal size. After 10 minutes add meatballs in soup, add salt. Close the slow cooker with a lid and keep on boiling in «Soup» mode for more than 10 minutes.

5. Five minutes later, turn off the slow cooker. Rinse fresh dill with running water, shake off excess liquid and chop. Add chopped dill greens to the soup, close the lid and let the soup stand for a few more minutes.

6. Serve with fresh greenery and fresh bread.

Stew pork with prunes

Preparation time: 30 minutes
Servings: 4
Kcal: 280

Net carbs: 9g / 0.31 oz / Fats: 21 g /0.74 oz / Proteins: 16g / 0.56 oz

Ingredients:

- 2 cups / 500ml
- 2 onion
- Pepper
- 1 ¼ / 150g prunes
- 35 oz. /1 kg pork
- 2tbsp. / 30 ml tomato sauce
- Vegetable oil

Preparation steps:

1. Rinse meat, pat with paper towel and cut into small pieces. Chop onion. In the slow cooker, turn on the «Frying» mode. Pour sunflower oil into the slow cooker bowl and put the meat after heating. Leave the lid open, stir the meat and wait for the liquid to boil.
2. Add onion and fry until well browned.
3. Put tomato paste in the meat, stir and fry a little together, after turn off the "Frying" program.
4. Add previously washed prunes, add to meat, and pour water, season salt and pepper. Cook on «Stewing» mode for 1.5 hour.
5. Serve with rice.

Turkey chili

Preparation time: 6 hours
Servings: 6
Kcal: 206

Net carbs: 4g / 0.14oz / Fats: 5g / 0.17oz / Proteins: 36 g / 1.26oz

Ingredients:

- 2 lbs. /900g turkey
- 2tsp. / 30 ml olive oil
- 1tsp./ 6g garlic powder
- 1 chopped onion
- 28oz/ 800g tomatoes
- ¾ cup / 180ml chicken broth
- 38oz / 1L tomato sauce
- 2tbsp. / 10g chili powder
- 2tbsp./
- Salt, pepper
- 30oz / 2 cans beans

Preparation steps:

1. Preheat the olive oil in a slow cooker bowl. Put turkey and strew with salt and pepper. Cook turkey until it soft and golden.
2. Turn on «Frying» mode. Add onion in a frying pan and roast for 3-4 minutes. Add garlic and fry for 1 minute.
3. Place turkey in a slow cooker; add tomatoes, tomato sauce, chicken broth, chili powder, smoked paprika, sugar and salt.
4. Stir properly.
5. Cook on low for 6 hours. Add the beans and cook for another 20 minutes, until the beans are warm. Add toppings if desired.

Chicken tortilla soup

Preparation time: 3hours
Servings: 4
Kcal: 375

Net carbs: 37g / 1.30 oz / Fats: 8g / 0.28oz / Proteins: 42g / 1.48 oz

Ingredients:

- 🍽 1/2 cup 15/ 80g diced white onions
- 🍽 1/2 cup / 90g red pepper, diced
- 🍽 15 oz. / 425g black beans can be washed and strained
- 🍽 1 cup/ 180g frozen corn
- 🍽 1 1/4 lbs / 600g Chicken breasts without skin
- 🍽 1 4 oz. /can soft green pepper
- 🍽 1 tsp./ cumin
- 🍽 1/2 tsp./ garlic powder
- 🍽 1 8 oz. /can of tomato sauce
- 🍽 1 14.5 oz./ cubed tomatoes do not drain
- 🍽 2 tsp. / chili powder
- 🍽 6 glasses chicken broth
- 🍽 1 tsp. / kosher salt
- 🍽 1 cup strips cake or more if desired
- 🍽 2 tbsp. / cilantro leaves crushed
- 🍽 Toppings such as sour cream, avocado, olives and shredded cheese

Preparation steps:

1. Place in a slow cooker bell pepper, corn, chicken, tomatoes, garlic powder, chicken broth, salt and other ingredients. Mix everything thoroughly to unite all ingredients.
2. Cover the low cooker and cook on low 6-8 hours/3-4 hours on high.
3. Take out chicken breasts and shred. Bring back in a slow cooker.
4. Stir in the chopped cilantro and ladle into bowls. Top with tortilla strips and any other toppings you desire. Serve immediately.

Taco

Preparation time: 3 hours
Servings: 5
Kcal: 150

Net carbs: 4g / 0.14oz / Fats: 2g / 0.07oz / Proteins: 22g / 0.77oz

Ingredients:

- 15oz / 450 g ground beef
- 1 tbsp. / 17ml olive oil
- 15oz / 450 g frozen vegetable mix for tacos
- 2cups / 400 g Ranch sauce
- 28 oz / 800 g canned beans
- 1 can of canned corn
- 2 cups / 400 g tomato sauce
- 2 tbsp. / 30ml water
- 14oz / 400 g diced tomato
- 1 green chili, chopped

Preparation steps:

1. Fry the minced meat in a cast iron skillet in olive oil until brown - 5-7 minutes. Add ranch sauce to the meat, mix and cook for another 1-2 minutes. Put the meat in a slow cooker.
2. Add the rest of the ingredients. Drain the juice from the corn. Set the Cooking or Slow Cooking mode to 3 hours.
3. Serve the puff dish with crispy toasts.

Lamb stew with squash

Preparation time: 1 hour
Servings: 7
Kcal: 156

Net carbs: 5g /0.17 oz / Fats: 13g / 0.45oz / Proteins: 7 g /0.24 oz

Ingredients:

- 2.2lbs / Lamb 1 kg
- 2 onions
- 1 garlic clove
- 5oz / 150g squash
- 2 carrots
- 1 1/3 cup / 200g green peas
- 3 potato
- 1 beef stock cube
- 4tbsp. / 60g butter
- Salt, pepper
- Fresh sage leaves

Preparation steps:

1. Peel potato, carrot and pumpkin. Dice. Chop garlic.
2. Wash and pat meat with paper towel. Cut into 8 parts.
3. Put butter in the slow cooker, set the "Multi-cook" mode, temperature 160 ° C, time 20 minutes. Put the mutton in the heated oil and roast on all sides for 10 minutes. Take out the meat from the slow cooker.

4. Put onion and garlic in a slow cooker bowl and fry until golden. Return the meat, pour in the broth, salt, season with pepper and close the lid. Set the "Multi-cook" mode, temperature 160 ° C, / 320 °F time for 1 hour.

5. Open the slow cooker, add vegetables, add a little broth if necessary and proceed cooking in the same mode for another 30 minutes.

6. Add green pea pods and finely chopped sage leaves, cook another 10 minutes in the same mode.

Desserts/snacks

Pie with dried fruits

Preparation time: 2 hours
Servings: 5
Kcal: 190

Net carbs: 42g / 1.48 oz / Fats: 7g / 0.24 oz / Proteins: 4g / 0.14oz

Ingredients:

- 2 1/3 cups / 320g flour
- 1 cup / 250 ml black tea
- 3tbsp. / 45ml sunflower oil
- 2 cups / 300gdried fruits +nuts
- 3tbsp / 50g any jam

- 1 cup / 200g sugar
- 1.5 tsp. / 10g baking powder
- 1tsp./ 10g vanilla sugar
- Sugar powder

Preparation steps:

1. Brew black tea. Combine tea, jam and sugar. Shuffle thoroughly.
2. Add sift flour, vanilla, salt, vegetable oil and baking powder.
3. Soak dried fruits previously. Chop dried fruits and nuts. Coat them in flour.
4. Add dried fruits and nuts in batter. Consistency is like thick sour cream.
5. Grease the slow cooker bowl with vegetable oil and pour the batter into it.
6. Bake in «Baking» mode until cooked. Time depends on the power of the slow cooker for about 90 minutes.
7. Take out the ready pie from the slow cooker, let cool.
8. Sprinkle with sugar powder.

Stuffed apples with cottage cheese

Preparation time: 50 minutes
Servings: 4
Kcal: 102

Net carbs: 11g / 0.38 oz / Fats: 4g / 0.14 oz / Proteins: 5g / 0.17 oz

Ingredients:

- 🍽 4 Apples
- 🍽 1 1/8 cup / 250g Cottage cheese
- 🍽 1 Egg Yolk
- 🍽 2tbsp. / 50g Sugar
- 🍽 1tsp. / 5g Cinnamon
- 🍽 Vanillin
- 🍽 1/3 cup / 50g Raisins
- 🍽 Nuts(optional)

Preparation steps:

1. Using a whisk, beat the yolk with sugar. Rub the cottage cheese through a sieve. Mix it with the yolk-sugar mass, add cinnamon and vanillin there, and raisins soaked in boiling hot water in advance.
2. Gently cut the core of the apples with sharp ones so as not to pierce the apples through. Fill them with cottage cheese. Put the stuffed apples in the slow cooker bowl, cook in the "Baking" or "Multicook" mode for half an hour.
3. Ready dessert can be served with homemade berry jam or cold sour cream.

Lemon Cake

Preparation time: 90minutes
Servings: 10
Kcal: 335

Net carbs: 40g / 1.41 oz / Fats: 17g / 0.59 oz / Proteins: 6g / 0.21 oz

Ingredients:

- 🍽 3 cups / 375g flour
- 🍽 1 cup / 250g butter
- 🍽 1 ¾ cup / 350g sugar powder
- 🍽 1/2 cup / 150g sour cream
- 🍽 3 lemons
- 🍽 6 eggs
- 🍽 1 cup / 70g coconut flakes
- 🍽 ½ cup / 100g sugar
- 🍽 10g baking powder

Preparation steps:

1. Beat soft butter of a room temperature with sugar powder to fluffy white consistency. One by one add gradually 6 eggs after each beat for 1 minute.
2. Remove zest from lemon, squeeze lemon juice and add in batter together with sour cream.
3. Stir thoroughly, add 50g coconut flakes .Sieve flour and baking powder. Mix everything properly.

4. Grease slow cooker bowl and sprinkle with flour. Lay out the dough and flatten. Cook in the "Baking" mode for about 80 minutes, check the readiness with a wooden stick, it should come out of the middle of the cake dry. Allow the cake to cool slightly in the slow cooker. After, turn it over gently on the grill.

5. For lemon caramel: mix in a saucepan 100g sugar, juice of half a lemon. Bring to boil and cook for about 2 minutes. Poke a cupcake with a stick through all cake.

6. Pour over caramel.

7. Sprinkle with coconut flakes.

Carrot cake

Preparation time: 70 minutes
Servings: 10
Kcal: 313

Net carbs: 32g / 1.12 oz / Fats: 6g / 0.21 oz / Proteins: 7g / 0.24 oz

Ingredients:

- 2 ¼ cup / 250g grated carrot
- 3 eggs
- 2 cups / 250g flour
- 1 cup / 200g sugar
- 1 cup / 200 ml vegetable oil
- 1 1/3 cup / 300g cream cheese
- ½ cup / 100g sugar powder
- 1tsp. / Cinnamon
- 2 g / Ginger
- Vanilla extract

Preparation steps:

1. Beat sugar with vegetable oil. One by one add eggs with non-stop beating.
2. Sieve flour, cinnamon ,ginger and baking powder to eggs mixture
3. Add grated carrot in dough. Mix well.
4. Grease slow cooker bowl with butter and powder with flour. Pour batter in a bowl. Turn on the «Baking» mode for 50 minutes. Check readiness with wooden stick.
5. Gently take out the cake from the slow cooker and let cool. Cut into half.
6. Mix cream cheese with a whisk, powdered sugar, vanilla seeds and butter.
7. Slather the lower bottom of the cake with half of cream.
8. Cover with a second cake and spread with the remaining cream. Put the cake in the refrigerator for 1 hour.
9. Garnish with walnuts.

Plum jam

Preparation time: 3 hours
Servings: 10
Kcal: 164

Net carbs: 46g / 1.62 oz / Fats: 0g / 0 oz / Proteins: 1g / 0.03 oz

Ingredients:

- 🍴 3.5 lbs. / 1.5kg plums
- 🍴 2.2 lbs. / 1kg sugar
- 🍴 2 sticks cinnamon

Preparation steps:

1. Remove the seeds from the plums and cut them into quarters.
2. Put the plums in the slow cooker and add sprinkle with sugar. Add cinnamon. Shuffle.
3. Cook in the Multi-Cook mode at 80 °/ 176 °F for 1 hour. Then mix.
4. Then cook in the «Multi-cook» mode at a temperature of 90°/194 °F for 2 hours. Shuffle.
5. Mash with a hand blender.
6. Pour hot jam into sterilized jars, roll up with sterilized lids and wrap until cool. Store at room temperature.

Keto recipes

Keto bread with pumpkin

Preparation time: 75 minutes
Servings: 10
Kcal: 118

Net carbs: 8g / 0.28 oz / Fats: 9g / 0.31oz / Proteins: 5g / 0.17 oz

Ingredients:

- 1 cup / 125g almond flour
- 3 eggs
- 50g / 25g pumpkin puree
- 50ml / 2tbsp. coconut milk
- 25g sesame / 1tbsp. flour
- 25g / 1tbsp. granulated natural sweetener
- 2tsp. / 8g baking powder
- 0.5tsp./ 1g salt

Preparation steps:

1. Sieve flour, sweetener, salt and baking powder in a big bowl.
2. Stir in pumpkin puree and coconut milk.
3. In a separate bowl whisk egg whites until tough fluffy consistency.
4. 1/3 of whipped whites stir in dough and then the rest stir gradually and gently.
5. Lubricate the slow cooker with coconut oil. Place dough inside, sprinkle with pistachio nuts, turn on «Baking» mode and cook for 40-50 minutes.

Keto prawns

Preparation time: 15 minutes
Servings: 6
Kcal: 270

Net carbs: 4g / 0.14 oz / Fats: 22 g /0.77 oz / Proteins: 15g / 0.52 oz

Ingredients:

- 17oz / 500g prawns
- 2 eggs
- ½ cup / 60g coconut flour
- ½ cup / 100g coconut oil
- 1tsp./ 6g Cajun seasoning

Preparation steps:

1. Prepare the Cajun seasoning: in a dry bowl mix 2 teaspoons of salt, 2 teaspoons of garlic powder, 2 teaspoons of paprika, 1 teaspoon of ground black pepper, onion powder, cayenne pepper, dried oregano, dried thyme and ½ teaspoon of red pepper.
2. Beat the eggs in a small bowl; in another bowl, mix coconut flour, salt and spices. Dip each shrimp in an egg, then in a mixture of coconut flour.
3. Grease slow cooker with coconut oil, turn on frying mode. Fry the shrimps for 5 minutes on each side in small portions. Put the finished shrimp on a paper towel to absorb extra fat.
4. Serve with vegetable salad.

Keto pizza with mushrooms

Preparation time: 25 minutes
Servings: 2
Kcal:

Net carbs: 7g / 0.24oz / Fats: 110g /3.38 oz / Proteins: 27 g / 0.95 oz

Ingredients:

- 🍽 2eggs
- 🍽 2tbsp. / 40g mayonnaise
- 🍽 ½ cup / 60g almond flour
- 🍽 1tbsp. / 25g flaxseed flour
- 🍽 1tsp. / 5g baking powder
- 🍽 Salt, pepper

- 🍽 7/8 cup / 60g mushrooms
- 🍽 1tbsp. /25g pesto
- 🍽 2tbsp./ 30ml olive oil
- 🍽 2,5 tbsp./ 45g sour cream
- 🍽 ½ cup / 45g Parmesan cheese

Preparation steps:

1. Mix eggs and mayonnaise with a mixer. Then, add flour, flaxseed flour ,baking powder, salt and mix thoroughly

2. Cover the baking tray with parchment, put the dough on it and with a spatula form a circle about 1 cm thick

3. Bake the base for 10 minutes in a preheated 180 ° C / 350°F oven. Take out from the oven .Let cool for 3-5 minutes

4. Combine chopped mushrooms, pesto, olive oil and sour cream. Put the mixture on the base, sprinkle with Parmesan and send back to the oven for another 5-10 minutes

5. Serve with chopped parsley.

Keto Risotto

Preparation time: 30 minutes
Servings: 4
Kcal: 455

Net carbs: 17g / 0.59 oz / Fats: 36g / 1.26 oz / Proteins: 15g / 0.52 oz

Ingredients:

- 21oz / 600g Cauliflower
- 1 cup / 100g Cheddar Cheese
- 1 1/3 cup / 100g mushrooms
- ½ cup / 50g walnuts
- ½ cup / 100 ml milk
- ¼ cup / 50 ml water
- 3 garlic cloves
- 2tbsp./ 30 ml olive oil
- 2tbsp./ 30g butter
- 1.5tsp./7g rosemary
- 1.5tsp./ paprika
- Salt

Preparation steps:

1. Preheat the oven to 200 ° C / 392°F and place the foil on the baking tray. Slice mushrooms, and combine them with chopped garlic, rosemary, walnuts and paprika in a small bowl and sprinkle with olive oil. Stir well to coat and dust with salt.

2. Spread the mixture evenly on a baking tray and bake in the oven for 15 minutes. Grind the top of the cauliflower in a blender

3. Steam the processed cauliflower in a medium-sized saucepan, under the lid, with 50 ml of water until the mixture is somewhat soft

4. Pour milk into a ladle and warm for a maximum of three minutes. Add Cheddar and butter, reduce the temperature to low and stir until the mixture is thick and uniform. Strew with salt to taste.

5. Take out the pan from the oven when the mushrooms are soft and their edges darken.

6. Serve the cauliflower risotto hot with the mushroom mixture on top. Add olive oil if desired.

Keto casserole Teriyaki with chicken

Preparation time: 2 hours
Servings: 6
Kcal: 300

Net carbs: 7g / 0.24 oz / Fats: 16g /0.56 oz / Proteins: 33g / 1.16 oz

Ingredients:

- 1 tsp./ 7g Ground ginger
- 1tsp./ 7g garlic powder
- 1tbsp./9ml rice vinegar
- ½ cup / 80 ml soy sauce
- 1tsp. / 7g chia seeds
- ½ cup / 100ml water
- 2tbsp. / 25 ml olive oil
- 6 chicken breasts
- 14 oz / 400g cauliflower
- 1 cup / 50g carrot
- 5/8 cup / 100g broccoli

Preparation steps:

1. In a big bowl mix ginger, garlic and vinegar, water and soy sauce.
2. Combine chia seeds with olive oil and add in sauce. Stir thoroughly until it homogeneous and thick.
3. Place diced chicken breasts, broccoli, cauliflower and cut into rings carrot.
4. Pour all teriyaki sauce, mix, cook in a slow cooker on low for 2 hours or until chicken is soft.

Pumpkin soup

Preparation time: 40 minutes
Servings: 6
Kcal: 199

Net carbs: 4g / 0.14 oz / Fats: 12g / 0.42 oz / Proteins: 2 g / 0.07 oz

Ingredients:

- 18oz / 500 g of pumpkin
- 1/2 chicken
- 2 garlic cloves
- ½ cup / 100 g butter
- 1 onion

Preparation steps:

1. Boil broth. Add salt and pepper to taste. Place ready chicken on the plate. Peel the pumpkin from seeds and skin.
2. Peel the onion and cut it into 4 slices, peel the garlic
3. Lay on a baking sheet large pieces of pumpkin, onion slices and garlic cloves. Put in a preheated oven (200 ° C) for about 20 minutes.
4. Bring the broth to a boil, add baked pumpkin, onion, garlic and chicken meat to it. Diminish the heat to medium and let the soup cook for another 15 minutes. Check for spices, at this step it's time to adjust the salt and pepper.
5. Remove the pan from the heat, let the soup cool slightly (about 20 minutes) After, mash it with a hand blender
6. Add butter at the very end.

Garlic chicken

Preparation time: 4 hours
Servings: 4
Kcal: 542

Net carbs: 9g /0.31 oz / Fats: 35g / 1.23 oz / Proteins: 45g /1.58 oz

Ingredients:

- 4 big chicken breasts
- 6 garlic cloves
- 1 cup / 200 ml heavy cream
- 1/3 cup / 120 ml Chicken broth
- 3/4 cup / 75g grated Parmesan
- 1 tbsp. / 15 ml Olive oil
- 1/2 cup /25g dried tomatoes (chopped)
- 2 cups / 400g spinach (sliced, packed)
- 1 tbsp. / 7g Italian seasoning
- Sea salt, ground pepper

Preparation steps:

1. Warm up the olive oil in a saucepan over medium heat.
2. Add garlic Sauté several minutes until is flavor. Add heavy cream and broth. Bring to a slight boil. Cook over low heat for 10 minutes.
3. Place chicken breasts in a slow cooker bowl. Top with Italian seasoning, sea salt and black pepper. Put dried tomatoes on the top. When the sauce is ready, simmer but not stew. Add grated cheese ¼ cup until homogeneous consistency. Pour the sauce over chicken. Cook for about 3-4 hours on high. Turn off the slow cooker add spinach. Stir.

Creamy chicken

Preparation time: 6 hours
Servings: 4
Kcal: 312

Net carbs: 7g / 0.24 oz / Fats: 12g / 0.42 oz / Proteins: 33g / 1.16 oz

Ingredients:

- 4 chicken breasts
- 1 1/3 cup / 100g fried mushrooms
- 1cup / 200ml red wine
- Salt, pepper
- ½ cup / 100ml heavy whipping cream

Preparation steps:

1. Pour oil in a slow cooker bowl and grease around the base.
2. Place chicken on the bottom.
3. Throw mushrooms, seasonings and pour wine on the top.
4. Cover with a lid. Cook on high 3-4 hours.
5. Take out the chicken and mushrooms from the slow cooker and put aside.
6. Stir in cream in a slow cooker's content. Stir well until is thick.
7. Return kitchen to a slow cooker and keep on cooking for 30 minutes.

Beef stroganoff

Preparation time: 30 minutes
Servings: 4
Kcal: 477

Net carbs: 7g / 0.24 oz / Fats: 34g / 1.19 oz / Proteins: 36g / 1.26 oz

Ingredients:

- 18oz / 500g minced beef
- 8oz / 250g mushrooms
- 1 cup /250 ml sour cream
- 2tbsp. / 30g butter
- 1 garlic clove
- Salt, pepper
- 1tbsp./ 15 ml lemon juice
- Chopped parsley

Preparation steps:

1. Turn the «Frying» mode. Add butter, when it melts add chopped garlic. Cook until flavor. After, add minced beef. Season with salt and pepper. Place ready cooked minced beef and put aside.

2. Drain extra fat, leave a little for mushrooms. Cook mushrooms in a «Frying» mode. Add several tablespoons of water and cook until soft. Set aside.

3. Pour sour cream into a pan. Add cooked beef, mushrooms and mix. Add lemon juice and parsley. Turn «Stewing» mode and cook for 5-10 minutes.

4. Garnish with greenery.

Almond Keto cake

Preparation time: 1 hour
Servings: 8
Kcal: 455

Net carbs: 5g / 0.17oz / Fats: 41g / 1.44oz / Proteins: 15g /0.52 oz

Ingredients:

- 1 cup / 140g almond flour
- 1/3 cup / 70g coconut flour
- 1 tbsp./ 15g melted butter
- 4 eggs
- 1tsp. / 4ml vanilla extract
- 1tsp. / 5g lemon zest
- Salt, a pinch

- 1 tsp. / 7g baking powder
- ½ cup / 110g cream cheese
- Sugar sweetener
- Glazing
- 1/2 cup / 100ml cream
- Raspberry

Preparation steps:

1. Beat eggs with salt, zest, vanilla, sweetener and cream cheese. Add flour and baking powder.
2. In the end, add cold butter.
3. Grease slow cooker bowl with butter.
4. Pour batter and cook in Baking mode for 1 hour.
5. Check the readiness with wooden stick.
6. Whisk cream and add raspberry.
7. Glaze the cake after it is completely cooled down.

Low carb recipes

Spicy prawns

Preparation time: 30 minutes
Servings: 12
Kcal: 67

Net carbs: 1g / 0.03 oz / Fats: 5g / 0.17 oz / Proteins: 6g / 0.21 oz

Ingredients:

- 24 peeled prawns
- 2tsp. / 10g fresh fennel
- 1tsp. /8g red pepper flakes
- Lemon Juice

- Zest of 2 lemons
- 4garlic cloves
- ¼ cup / 60ml olive oil

Preparation steps:

1. Turn «Frying» mode. In a separate bowl place prawns, sprinkle with fennel, zest of 2 lemons. Add garlic, olive oil and mix everything with hands to coat evenly all prawns.
2. Fry until prawns are pink. Splash with lemon juice and serve.

Chicken salad with grapes and curry

Preparation time: 55 minutes
Servings: 4
Kcal: 325

Net carbs: 13g / 0.45oz / Fats: 14g / 0.49 oz / Proteins: 37g /1.30 oz

Ingredients:

- 21oz / 600g chicken breasts
- 5oz / 150g salad mixture
- 1 cup / 250ml chicken broth
- 1 cup / 250ml water
- ¼ cup / 35g almond chopped
- ½ cup /125ml yogurt
- 2tbsp./30g mayonnaise
- 1tsp. / 6g curry powder
- 1 cup / 100g grapes
- 1tbsp. / 17 ml olive oil
- ¼ cup / 50g chopped cilantro
- 1tsp. / 8ml lemon juice

Preparation steps:

1. In a middle-sized saucepan mix water with broth and bring to boil. Add chicken and stew 8 minute under a covered lid. Turn off the cooker and leave chicken for 20 minutes in this liquid. After, take out and let cool and cut into small cubes.
2. Fry almond for 3 minutes until aroma.
3. In a separate bowl combine yogurt, mayonnaise and curry powder. Add chicken, cilantro and strew with salt and pepper.
4. In a big bowl mix greenery with lemon juice, oil, salt and pepper.
5. Serve in portion plates, topped with almond.

Pork tenderloin

Preparation time: 35 minutes
Servings: 4
Kcal: 209

Net carbs: 2g / 0.07 oz / Fats: 9g / 0.31 oz / Proteins: 30g / 1.05 oz

Ingredients:

- 21oz / 600g pork tenderloin
- 1tbsp. / 15ml olive oil
- 1tsp. / 3g garlic powder
- 1tsp. / 3g dried oregano
- 1tsp. / 3g cumin
- 1 tsp. / 3g chopped garlic
- 1 tsp. / 3g cilantro
- 1tsp. / 3g thyme
- Salt

Preparation steps:

1. In a separate bowl mix all dry ingredients. Rub meat with this dry seasoning.
2. In a big skillet fry pork tenderloin for about 10 minutes from each side on olive oil.
3. Turn on «Stewing» mode. Transfer meat in a slow cooker and cook for 2 hours.

Marinated chicken breasts

Preparation time: 45 minutes
Servings: 4
Kcal: 327

Net carbs: 3g / 0.10 oz / Fats: 16g /0.56 oz / Proteins: 40 g / 1.41oz

Ingredients:

- 4 Chicken breasts
- 2tbsp. / 30ml apple vinegar
- 1-3tsp. / 8g dried herbs
- 1-2tbsp. / 30g mustard
- 1-2tsp. / 7g onion powder
- ¼ cup / 60ml olive oil

Preparation steps:

1. In a large plastic bag with zip lock, mix vinegar, herbs, mustard onion powder. Close the bag and shake to mix all the ingredients evenly. Then open the bag put the chicken breast in the marinade. Close and shake the bag to evenly cover the whole chicken.
2. Turn on frying mode. Place chicken in a slow cooker and fry for 4 minutes from each side. Then change the mode into Stewing and cook for 45 minutes.
3. Serve with pesto sauce.

Stirfry

Preparation time: 40 minutes
Servings: 6
Kcal: 166

Net carbs: 15g / 0.52 oz /Fats: 9g / 0.31 oz / Proteins: 19g / 0.67oz

Ingredients:

- 10oz / 300g Turkey fillet
- 1 packet Buckwheat noodles soba
- 1 packet Chinese Frozen Vegetable Mix
- 1/2 cup 120ml Teriyaki sauce.
- ¼ cup / 60ml Refined sunflower oil (soybean or corn)
- 3 tbsp. / 40ml Hot chili sauce.
- Chives – for serving

Preparation steps:

1. Cut turkey fillet into thin slices. Add teriyaki sauce and put aside for 40 minutes for marinating.
2. Turn on the «Stewing» mode for 15 minutes. Pour in slow cooker sunflower oil. Put vegetable mixture. Close the lid and cook to the end of mode.
3. After «Stewing» turn on «Frying» mode for 15 minutes. Add in a slow cooker bowl turkey meat with marinade and spicy sauce. Stirring cook for 10 minutes
4. Cook in advance soba. Add prepared buckwheat pasta to meat and keep on frying, continuously stirring.
5. Serve with chopped chives.

Broccoli cream soup

Preparation time: 45 minutes
Servings: 4
Kcal: 160

Net carbs: 15g / 0.52 oz /Fats: 9g / 0.31 oz / Proteins: 17g / 0.59oz

Ingredients:

- 1 middle-sized onion
- 1 celery stalk
- 2 garlic cloves
- 1tbsp./ 15 ml olive oil
- 1tbsp./ 15g butter
- 1tsp./ 3g thyme
- 21oz / 600g broccoli
- 2 cups / 500ml water
- 4cups / 1L chicken stock
- Salt, pepper

Preparation steps:

1. Turn on frying mode, pour olive oil and butter, and melt. Add chopped onion and celery stalk. Cook until is soft stirring from now and then. Add chopped garlic and fresh thyme. Add broccoli, water and stock. Bring to boil. After cover the lid and cook in Soup mode 20 minutes.
2. Liquidize soup in a food processor to homogeneous consistency. Add salt and pepper to taste.

Fritata

Preparation time: 2 hours
Servings: 8
Kcal: 166

Net carbs: 5g / 0.17 oz / Fats: 12g / 0.42oz / Proteins: 10g / 0.35 oz

Ingredients:

- 5 oz /150g baby kale
- 6oz / 175g roasted bell pepper
- 5oz / 150g crumbled feta
- 3tbsp./ 45ml olive oil
- 8 eggs
- 1/2tsp. / 2g seasoning blend
- 1/3 cup / chives

Preparation steps:

1. Turn frying mode. Heat up the olive oil in a slow cooker. When oil is well warmed up, sauté until it's softened for 3-4 minutes.

2. Spray slow cooker bowl with non-stick spray or olive oil. Transfer prepared kale cabbage. Change the mode Low.

3. Slice, chives, bell pepper and feta. Add to cabbage.

4. Beat eggs well, and pour in a slow cooker. Season with spices. Cook on low 2-3 hours.

Salmon with herbs

Preparation time: 1 hour
Servings: 6
Kcal: 187

Net carbs: 1g / 0.03 oz /Fats: 11g / 0.38 oz / Proteins: 20g / 0.70oz

Ingredients:

- 6 salmon fillet
- 2 cups / 500ml water
- 1 cup / 250ml white dry wine
- 1 shallot

- 5-6 sprigs parsley
- 1 lemon
- Sea salt, ground pepper
- 1 bay leaf

Preparation steps:

1. Mix water, wine, lemon, shallot, bay leaf, greenery salt and pepper. Cook on high for 30 minutes.
2. Rub salmon top with salt and pepper. Transfer in a slow cooker skin down. Cook on low until salmon is soft.
3. Serve with lemon slices.

Lemon low carb cake

Preparation time: 2 hours
Servings: 8
Kcal: 350

Net carbs: 6g / 0.21 oz / Fats: 84g / 2.96 oz / Proteins: 8g / 0.28 oz

Ingredients:

- 🍽 2 eggs
- 🍽 1 ½ cup / 180g almond flour
- 🍽 2tsp. / 11g baking powder
- 🍽 Lemon zest(2 lemons)
- 🍽 6tbsp. / 75g organic sweetener

- 🍽 ½cup / 120g melted butter
- 🍽 ½ cup / 100g whipping cream
- 🍽 ½ cup / 120ml coconut oil
- 🍽 2 tbsp./ 30ml lemon juice

Topping

- 🍽 3tbsp. / 35g sweetener
- 🍽 ½ cup / 125ml boiling water

- 🍽 2tbsp. / 40g melted butter
- 🍽 2tbsp./ 32ml lemon juice

Preparation steps:

1. Combine all dry ingredients in a big bowl.
2. Whisk whipping cream, butter, zest, lemon juice and eggs in a single bowl.
3. Stir wet mix into dry and combine until homogeneous consistency. Pour batter in a slow cooker previously greased with butter.
4. Mix all topping ingredients in a bowl and pour over cake butter in a slow cooker. Cover and cook on high 2-3 hours. If you insert a wooden stick in center, it comes out dry. That means that the cake is ready.
5. Serve warm with favorite fruits and whipped cream.

Shepherd's pie

Preparation time: 6 hours
Servings: 10
Kcal: 183

Net carbs: 7g / 0.24 oz /Fats: 6g / 0.21 oz / Proteins: 50 g / 1.76 oz

Ingredients:

- 1 cauliflower
- 1 onion
- 2 cups /150g mushrooms
- 1tbsp. / 5g garlic powder
- 2tbsp. / 50g coconut flour
- 2 lb / 850g ground turkey
- 2 zucchini
- 2 tomatoes
- ½ cup / 60g Parmesan
- Spices (dried thyme, paprika, parsley 1tsp.)

Preparation steps:

1. Chop and core the cauliflower. Rice it in a food processor.
2. In a big skillet sauté mushrooms and onions until transparent. Transfer in a slow cooker. Fry turkey in the same pan and transfer in a slow cooker. Add spices, tomatoes and zucchini as well and stir thoroughly. Layer riced cauliflower over the top mixture in a slow cooker. Sprinkle cheese and cook on low 3-4 hours.

Disclaimer

This book contains opinions and ideas of the author and is meant to teach the reader informative and helpful knowledge while due care should be taken by the user in the application of the information provided. The instructions and strategies are possibly not right for every reader and there is no guarantee that they work for everyone. Using this book and implementing the information/recipes therein contained is explicitly your own responsibility and risk. This work with all its contents, does not guarantee correctness, completion, quality or correctness of the provided information. Misinformation or misprints cannot be completely eliminated.

Design: Natalia Design

cover picture - Elena Eryomenko

Printed in Germany
by Amazon Distribution
GmbH, Leipzig

17593124R00066